PN
4784
.H46
1988

Exercises for
MEDIA WRITING
Second Edition

Bruce H. Hinson
University of Oklahoma

To accompany
MEDIA WRITING: PREPARING
INFORMATION FOR THE MASS MEDIA
Second Edition
by Doug Newsom
and James A. Wollert

Poynter Institute for Media Studies
Library

MAR 22 '88

Wadsworth Publishing Company
Belmont, California
A Division of Wadsworth, Inc.

©1988 by Wadsworth, Inc. All rights reserved. No part of this book may be reproduced, stored in a retrieval system, or transcribed, in any form or by any means, electronic, mechanical, photocopying, recording, or otherwise, without the prior written permission of the publisher, Wadsworth Publishing Company, Belmont, California 94002, a division of Wadsworth, Inc.

ISBN 0-534-08713-2

Printed in the United States of America

1 2 3 4 5 6 7 8 9 10—92 91 90 89 88

Contents

Preface   v

Part I   Introduction to Media Writing   1

Exercise 1   Storytelling (Chapter 1)   1
Exercise 2   Economical Storytelling (Chapter 1)   3
Exercise 3   Storytelling as News (Chapter 1)   5
Exercise 4   Making Change for Two-Dollar Words (Chapter 2)   7
Exercise 5   Translating Technical Information (Chapter 2)   9
Exercise 6   Organizing the Story (Chapter 2)   13
Exercise 7   The Oral Style (Chapter 2)   15
Exercise 8   Research for Reporting, Reporting on Research (Chapter 3)   17
Exercise 9   Getting, and Explaining, the Point (Chapter 3)   19

Part II   Writing Basics and Copy Formats   25

Exercise 10   Getting the Reader's Attention (Chapter 4)   25
Exercise 11   Leads for the Ear (Chapter 4)   27
Exercise 12   From Print to Broadcast (Chapter 4)   29
Exercise 13   Under the Umbrella (Chapter 4)   31
Exercise 14   Building a Story (Chapter 5)   33
Exercise 15   Quoting the Source (Chapter 5)   35
Exercise 16   More Notes and Quotes (Chapter 5)   37
Exercise 17   Facts and Figures (Chapter 5)   39
Exercise 18   Facts and Figures Out Loud (Chapter 5)   41
Exercise 19   Quotes on the Air (Chapter 5)   43
Exercise 20   Writing to Audiotape (Chapter 5)   45
Exercise 21   . . . and More Writing to Audiotape (Chapter 5)   47
Exercise 22   Words and Pictures (Chapter 5)   49
Exercise 23   Pictures and Words (Chapter 5)   51
Exercise 24   Writing for Videotex and Teletext (Chapter 6)   53
Exercise 25   More Videotex (Chapter 6)   55
Exercise 26   The Interview (Chapter 7)   57
Exercise 27   Multiple Interviews for a Single Story (Chapter 7)   59
Exercise 28   Combining Quotes for Broadcast (Chapter 7)   61
Exercise 29   Reporting Speeches (Chapter 8)   63

Part III   Complex Story Structures   65

Exercise 30   Covering the Speech (Chapter 8)   65
Exercise 31   After the Speech (Chapter 8)   67

Exercise 32	Covering Meetings (Chapter 9)	69
Exercise 33	Not All Meetings Are Alike (Chapter 9)	71
Exercise 34	Public Relations Writing as a Source (Chapter 10)	73
Exercise 35	Public Relations Writing That Gets Attention (Chapter 10)	77
Exercise 36	Promotion (Chapter 10)	79
Exercise 37	The "Atmosphere" Feature (Chapter 11)	81
Exercise 38	The Personality Feature (Chapter 11)	83
Exercise 39	The Whole versus the Sum of Its Parts (Chapter 11)	85
Exercise 40	The Feature on Radio (Chapter 11)	87
Exercise 41	Every Journalist a Columnist (Chapter 11)	89
Exercise 42	Depth Reporting (Chapter 12)	91
Exercise 43	The Depth of Controversy (Chapter 12)	93

Part IV Persuasive Writing 95

Exercise 44	Advertising: Selling an Image (Chapter 13)	95
Exercise 45	Advertising: Selling a Style (Chapter 13)	97
Exercise 46	Advertising: Hearing the Style (Chapter 13)	99
Exercise 47	Reviews: The Journalist as Interested Observer (Chapter 14)	101
Exercise 48	Reviews: The Journalist as "Insider" (Chapter 14)	103
Exercise 49	"Eds" and "Op-Eds" (Chapter 14)	105
Exercise 50	Editorials: The Last Word (Chapter 14)	107

Preface

This exercise book has been designed to give you an opportunity to work independently at the skills being introduced in the classroom. Most of the exercises require that you use local news media to ensure your exposure to the media for which you will be writing.

This book has been written to correlate with the 4 parts of your *Media Writing* text.

One element that couldn't be included is the practice you can get from *rewriting*. When your instructor returns your efforts, read the corrections and comments carefully, then rewrite the piece. You practice your tennis, piano and other such skills—practice writing!

PART I
Introduction to Media Writing

Exercise 1 Storytelling

(Chapter 1)

Journalism is akin to storytelling, describing or explaining an event, an object or a person to someone who was not there. Begin with a significant event in your life: your high school graduation, your first day in college or your first day on a job, for example. Imagine your description of that event as a conversation with a friend, attempting to relate in detail all of the significant facts, interesting sidelights and feelings involved. Write that "conversation" as you would speak it if you had your listener's undivided attention (at least to the extent of two double-spaced typed pages).

Grade or Score_____   Name/Date_____

Exercise 2 Economical storytelling (Chapter 1)

Assume the friend to whom you told that "significant event" isn't present, and you must relate the story in a letter. From your basic "conversational" account, condense the essentials of the story into a one-page double-spaced typed letter, remembering that you must clearly describe everything; your reader cannot prompt you with questions or non-verbal feedback.

Grade or Score____ Name/Date_____

Exercise 3 Storytelling as news   *(Chapter 1)*

Count the words in your letter from the preceding exercise. Rewrite the story in half as many words, with these changes that make the difference between storytelling and what we typically think of as news. Remove any personalization, that is, any reference to *I, we, you* and so on. In this version, describe the event as having happened to a third party; you are simply an observer and reporter.

Exercise 4 Making change for two-dollar words *(Chapter 2)*

The search for background information on a story may take the journalist on a long, complicated road. The journalist's job is to make the trip easier for the reader to follow.

Consider the following example of a piece of scholarly source material used for background in a story on the politics of the Middle East. It is good information, but hardly accessible to the average reader. Rewrite it in no more than three paragraphs, maintaining the important points.

Born of the revolutionary era of the late 18th century and the period of the Napoleonic wars, nationalism flourished and matured in a period and a place, Western Europe, where existing political divisions and a reasonably long continuity of such divisions had already contributed much to cultural and linguistic differentiation. Particularist nationalism in a political sense took root easily and prospered as an ideology. In the mid-19th century it flared up anew in Central Europe and then receded into the category of interesting but outdated historical phenomena, to be superseded by imperialism, the "mature" nationalism of a politically and economically powerful Europe.

Yet it was the original, inward-looking nationalism that Woodrow Wilson resurrected at Versailles almost half a century after the movement had supposedly died, and the two national ideologies must and did inevitably clash. Even before World War I had ended, Wilson stated as one of his principles for the solution of the vexing territorial questions which would be involved in the peace settlement ". . . that all well-defined national aspirations shall be accorded the utmost satisfaction that can be accorded them without introducing new or perpetuating old elements of discord and antagonism that would be likely in time to break the peace of Europe and consequently of the world."

It was clear, unequivocal declaration of intent to realize the worthy ambitions of subject populations in Europe and the Near East, a promise of fulfillment of sweeping idealistic pledges. One of the marks of political maturity of the new world order would be the creation of new sovereign national units, the visible expression of national self-consciousness, the political foundation of progress and prosperity, both material and spiritual. Like newly free nationalities everywhere, Arab patriots viewed with undisguised joy the prospect of that "coveted state of self-determination."

Yet dreams were destined to disillusionment, the ebullient prophets of the Arab political renascence were to be publicly disgraced, glowing optimism was to become first shocked disbelief, then bitter cynicism. But why the discrepancy between the hope and the realization? Had the would-be Arab states built their goals on false premises; had the structure of Arab national ambition grown too heavy for the factual assurances at its base? Or were the Western powers actually depriving the Arabs of their just reward; was the vilification and antagonism they were to face justified by their own duplicity?

Grade or Score_____ Name/Date_____

Exercise 5 Translating technical information   *(Chapter 2)*

The journalist as go-between must often translate information written for a specialized audience into a form understood by a general audience. From the following technical report, write a three-paragraph account in clear, non-technical language.

Gas Research Institute February 1987

TECHNOLOGY PROFILE

Pulse Combustion Griddle

Problem

Changing lifestyles in the United States have opened up new market opportunities for fast-food and full-service restaurants. This rapid growth of the food service market brings higher expectations for commercial cooking equipment capabilities. The gas-fired commercial griddle, though fairly simple in concept, must meet stringent performance requirements. It needs to be reliable, durable, and easy to use and clean. The griddle must cook food quickly and achieve consistent results. Increasingly, restaurant owners also want the griddle to be highly efficient, since roughly one-third of a restaurant's energy costs arise from food preparation.

GRI Solution

A pulse combustion griddle, under development by the American Gas Association Laboratories with GRI funding, will outperform conventional gas-fired griddles in efficiency, cooking, and product quality control.

Benefits

The pulse combustion griddle's efficiency exceeds 70 percent, a significant improvement over conventional griddles (less than 48 percent efficient) and infrared griddles (60 to 64 percent efficient). In practical terms, the pulse griddle cooks 360 quarter-pound hamburgers per hour at 72,000 Btu per hour input, while the conventional griddle needs a 90,000 Btu per hour input to accomplish the same task in the same amount of time. This increase in efficiency is expected to provide a 27 percent operating cost savings.

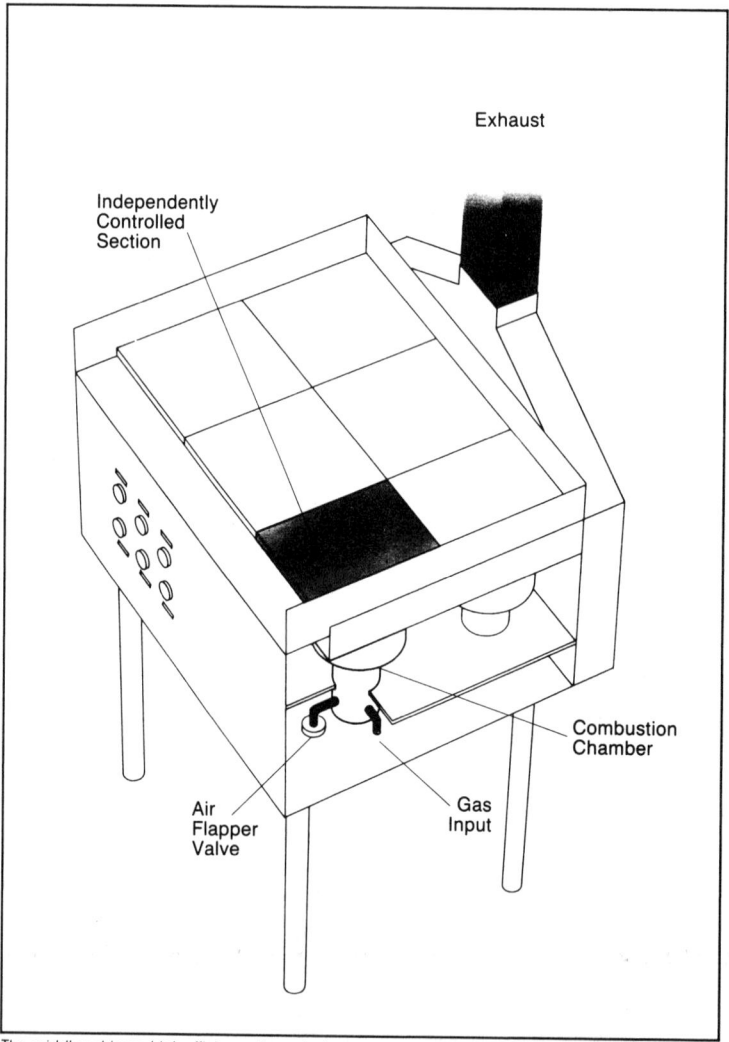

The griddle achieves high efficiency through six rectangular pulse combustion chambers beneath the griddle's surface.

10 / EXERCISE 5

Concept

The griddle integrates advanced pulse combustion technology and improved heat transfer with solid-state controls. The pulse combustion system differs from atmospheric burner systems in conventional gas-fired griddles. In the pulse process, air and gas are premixed in the combustion chamber. A spark plug ignites the initial combustion, creating a pressure pulse that closes off the air and fuel inlet valves. The pressure pulse forces combustion products through the combustor, scrubbing the underside of the griddle plate, and out the exhaust pipe into an exhaust decoupler. The resulting pressure drop draws in more fuel-air mixture for the next pulse, which is ignited by residual flames and heat from the previous combustion cycle. Once started, the process is self-perpetuating at approximately 35 cycles per second.

The griddle achieves high efficiency and temperature control through six unique rectangular pulse combustion chambers placed beneath the griddle's working surface area. The griddle's temperature varies no more than $\pm 10°F$ over most of its working surface from the 350°F thermostat setpoint, compared to variances of as much as $\pm 75°F$ for conventional equipment. This consistency results in better product quality control and favorably impacts cooking time.

The pulse griddle also offers cooking flexibility because the six combustors, operating with solid-state control systems, can be individually shut down or operated to match a given cooking load. Likewise, each section can be operated at a different temperature, thereby conserving energy and permitting the chef to cook several different types of food at the same time.

Project Status

In conjunction with the American Gas Association Laboratories, the

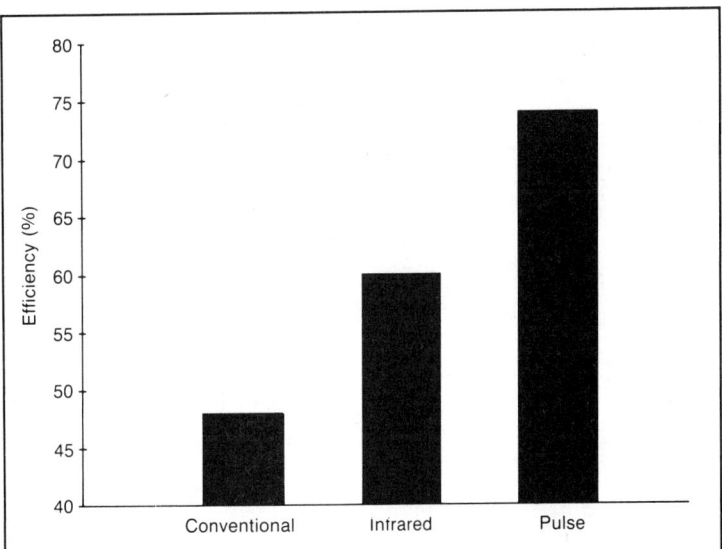

Griddle efficiency comparison.

participating manufacturer, Garland Commercial Industries, evaluated a laboratory prototype during early 1986 for efficiency, serviceability, cooking performance, and flexibility. Results from this evaluation were used in the design and construction of four prototype units which will undergo a year-long field test beginning in the first quarter of 1987. Testing will be conducted to verify the griddle's performance and reliability.

Prospectus

Assuming a successful field test, Garland expects to commercialize the pulse combustion griddle beginning in the first quarter of 1988. As a major manufacturer of commercial food service equipment, Garland's capabilities to manufacture and distribute the pulse combustion griddle will greatly facilitate its successful entry into the marketplace.

For Further Information, Contact:

Donald E. Fritzsche
Senior Project Manager,
Commercial Appliances

Renee M. Nault
Editor, Technical Communications

Gas Research Institute
8600 West Bryn Mawr Avenue
Chicago, Illinois 60631
312/399-8100

Grade or Score_____   Name/Date_____

Exercise 6 Organizing the story   (Chapter 2)

The organization of scattered facts into an easily understood form is as important as the language used in telling the story. A reporter took the following notes from a telephone conversation with the dispatcher at the local fire department. Turn them into a coherent story no longer than four paragraphs, emphasizing the most important and interesting facts first, as you would tell the story to the person in the next seat.

Fire in the north Lake Thunderbird area. Broke out yesterday afternoon. Burned 1,500 acres of brush and destroyed two houses east of 120th Street NE, up to 8 a.m. today. Out of control on a 5-mile front. Fire burning on a 20-mile perimeter. 500 firemen and volunteers on the fire line. They are from Norman, Moore, Purcell, Lexington and Little Axe communities. Norman Fire Chief Gerald Fuzzell says it's the worst fire in many years and the county's first major brush fire of the season. Weather conditions are bad. Temperatures in the 80s and low humidity and strong gusts of wind. Fire officials said there is danger that the fire will spread on all fronts unless there is a break in the dry, hot weather. Last night some 100 families were evacuated from the fire area. The two homes that were burned were vacant at the time they caught fire. The owners have not yet been identified. No injuries have been reported.

Grade or Score_____ Name/Date_____

Exercise 7 The oral style *(Chapter 2)*

A story to be heard follows rules different from those governing a story to be read. From the same notes used in Exercise 6, write a 35- to 40-second story in broadcast style. Concentrate on active voice and present tense where possible.

Exercise 8 Research for reporting, reporting on research

(Chapter 3)

Research for information on good stories frequently can lead to other research. Then the journalist's job becomes making information that's of interest to many people accessible to them. People generally are fascinated by computers, but how many would plow through the following story, and how many who did would thoroughly understand it? Your job as a reporter is to digest, restructure and simplify the important points, in a story of about 250 words.

Parallel processing research facility

By Doris Hinson

The buzzword in scientific computing is speed. As soon as a faster computer hits the market, researchers design more complex simulations—which in turn require a machine that computes with even more speed.

Problems that used to take many, many hours to solve on older computers can now be done in just a few hours, or mere minutes on a supercomputer. Some problems cannot even be investigated without a supercomputer. But with it, geologists can model reservoirs; astronomers can model the birth of stars and learn how galaxies are formed; atmospheric scientists can make long range weather forecasts; and biologists can study molecules to eventually find vaccines effective against viruses.

In the last few years, the computer which had the most power and speed became the supercomputer of that period. We are now at the point where the new supercomputers are called class seven supercomputers.

"The astounding progress in microelectronics has fueled a rapid growth in computer performance," says Dr. Julio Cesar Díaz, professor of computer science. "However, this progress is finally beginning to approach fundamental physical limitations."

Electrical signals traveling close to the speed of light can only move about 30 centimeters in 1 nanosecond (one billionth of a second). Current supercomputers presently run with times of about 10 nanoseconds. Projected models with times of 1 nanosecond must be built within a one-foot cube, and to attain a faster speed of models with times of 0.1 nanosecond would require an entire computer to be built in a one-inch cube.

"The obvious way to overcome these limitations is with parallel processors," Díaz says. "Parallelism consists of the coordination of several processors working at the same time on different portions of the same problem, enabling the results to be achieved in significantly less time.

"In the past few years, commercially available parallel processors have begun to appear," Díaz continues, "and these more advanced computers are setting the standards for the next generation of high performance computers."

Díaz and computer science professors Drs. Sudarshan K. Dhall and S. L. Lakshmivarahan are the initial members of the Parallel Processing Institute, dedicated to carrying out innovative research in various areas of parallel processing and supercomputers.

The university established the Oklahoma Parallel Processing Research Facility through a grant from the recently legislated More Oklahoma Science and Technology (MOST) fund. This fund was established with the support of the legislature and the governor and was provided to match funds provided by the National Science Foundation to help researchers in Oklahoma become more competitive for research support.

The facility is centered around the minisupercomputer FX/8, manufactured by the Alliant Computer System Corporation, which recently granted the facility additional components for the minisupercomputer. Díaz, Dhall, and Lakshmivarahan conduct their research activity on the Alliant, the first with the ability to automatically identify program sections that can be run in parallel.

The facility will enable the Parallel Processing Institute to foster innovative ideas for parallel processing and to provide the education and training needed by researchers who will use the next generation supercomputers. The facility is designed to meet the needs of the entire campus and will be used by researchers in areas such as mathematics, meteorology and physics.

"The facility is greatly invigorating parallel processing research at the University," Díaz says. "Activities include the development of parallel algorithms, methods for automatic detection of parallelism in serial programs, parallel programming languages, distributed data base, and others. The Institute has already developed parallel algorithms for the solution of mathematical systems arising in the simulation of enhanced oil recovery.

"It is not only less costly to develop experiments on the FX/8, but also easier," says Díaz. "The large supercomputers are meant for final production runs, not for interactive development. On the other hand, the Alliant FX/8 is designed so that interactive development is efficient; it does not sacrifice the computational power, which is independent."

The National Science Foundation recently awarded a grant to form a computer network of eight Midwest universities, including OU and Oklahoma State University. The award of $1 million will provide faculty researchers access to five supercomputer centers and will cover the cost for three years of providing leased dedicated telephone lines to connect the eight universities to the NSF supercomputer network.

The Oklahoma Parallel Processing Facility will assist faculty in other departments and schools to develop software programs intended for advanced NSF supercomputers, suitable for applications as varied as weather forecasting, geophysical prospecting, and oil recovery simulations. Investigators can now develop their research on the FX/8 and then move it across the network to a larger supercomputer.

Grade or Score_____ Name/Date_____

Exercise 9 Getting, and explaining, the point *(Chapter 3)*

Perhaps it helps to think of your job as finding not one but several needles of information in a verbal haystack. They are worth finding and relaying to others, but it takes some digging. From the following research report on a perennial professional topic, come up with a one-page story of interest to the general reader.

Oklahoma Journalism Reports

April 1976 — A publication of the Journalism Research Center, H.H. Herbert School of Journalism, 860 Van Vleet Oval, Room 235, The University of Oklahoma. Norman, OK 73069. L. Edward Carter, Editor. — **No. 6**

How Oklahoma High School Journalism Students Look at the 'Journalistic Ethic'

By Bruce H. Hinson and Ernest F. Larkin

It is not news that news is news. Less cryptically, most practitioners, observers and consumers of journalism are more than ever aware of the public's interest in the processes of newsgathering and dissemination and particularly in the actions and character of journalists themselves. Hollywood professionals do not seem unduly concerned over recouping eight and one-half million dollars spent on "All the President's Men," which, for all its other powerful themes, is largely a dramatized documentary of the actions, thoughts and personalities of two reporters.

But Watergate is merely the latest incident in a series of events stretching back through the history of the United States that have focused unusual attention on the role of the press, not always to the credit of the institution. In most cases, there has been an implicit if not explicit assumption of the "power" of the press to influence society for better or for worse: yellow journalism, muckraking, the Pentagon papers, the "new" journalism that is announced cyclically through our history. This assumption of power inevitably raises the question of motivation: "What are 'they' trying to do to 'us' and why?"

The same question, phrased by a journalist about himself and his colleagues, might read: "What are 'we' trying to do 'them' and why?" That it is being asked is evident in the proliferation of journalism reviews and the formation of a national news council. Journalists appear to be, fortunately, as concerned about the "proper" performance of their function as the public in general.

But who is a journalist? Perhaps more importantly, what is a journalist? Is it a Bob Woodward or a Carl Bernstein? Is it Hildy Johnson of "The Front Page?" Is it the thinly disguised William Randolph Hearst of "Citizen Kane?" Obviously the answer will vary depending on the background and experience of the respondent; does he have intimate knowledge of working reporters or does he base his judgments on a composite of fictional characters created more for dramatic effect than accuracy?

The Problem

For the immediate purposes of this study, the authors chose to disregard the "source" of the "image." What was of more concern was the set of attitudes based upon that image, attitudes concerning the motivation of the relatively impersonal "journalist."

We were, in effect, trying to measure the "ethics" of the journalist as perceived by different groups. The term "ethics" itself is semantically slippery in spite of its common, almost casual usage, but for purposes of this study, the investigators framed statements around the working definition provided by philosopher of history R.G. Collingwood that "ethics" is "the theory of action."[1]

Methodology

Statements for the instrument were organized under eight different categories or facets relating to the actions of journalists: economic conflict of interest, personal conflict of interest, advocacy, social service versus personal gain, rights and privileges, personal behavior, withholding information and personal integrity. Under each category, respondents were asked to agree or disagree (on a five-point scale) with five statements ranging from the "pure" ethical position to the most unethical. Formulation of the categories and statements was refined through suggestions, discussion and pre-testing with an experimental intersession class (half of whom were non-journalism majors) studying the "image" of journalism. Under the first category for example, the questions might range from the "pure" form, "A journalist refuses to accept anything of material value from a news source," to "A journalist accepts anything; it's a fringe benefit."

The authors sought to measure two dimensions of these ethical attitudes: what the respondents thought journalists actually did and what they thought journalists should do. Therefore, with minimal change in wording, i.e., changing "is" to "ought to be", etc., a second set of 40 statements was administered immediately after the first. For this pilot study, the instrument was given a total of 37 high school students, members of first and second year journalism classes at a large high school in north central Oklahoma. The results were subjected to factor analysis.

Findings

THE 'IDEAL' JOURNALIST

Analysis of the data from the ethics statements indicates that while the respondents are basically in agreement concerning how the journalist should behave in regard to ethical questions they also have some basic differences in the importance they place on various kinds of ethical behavior.

In regard to the questions concerning their ideal ethical behavior the 37 respondents all tended to agree that the journalist should see his job as interesting and respectable, should display self confidence, and that he should not accept gifts from news sources.

However, when looking at the differences between these respondents a total of six different types of individuals can be identified based on their concern over the various dimensions included in the ethical statements.

Type 1 included 15 of the 37 respondents. These individuals indicate that they believe the ideal journalist should be honest, should attempt to counter his own views by seeking opposing views to publish, should report events in a calm manner and display self confidence. He should also cooperate with officials to withhold information which might affect public welfare and should adhere to the moral standards of his society. They also believe that he should work to advance the welfare of society rather than himself and should view his job as interesting and respectable.

Type 1 individuals also feel that the ideal journalist should not accept gifts from news sources, should not try to shock his audience or look at his job as a route to power. He should not promote his own views but should report all sides of the issue equally. Finally he should not be unethical or arrogant.

Type 2 individuals (three of the 37) differ from Type 1 in their perception of the personal behavior of the ideal journalist. They strongly agree that he should be basically honest but pushy and should display self-confidence. However, they also feel that he should be subject to stricter accountability for sources, facts and consequences of his reports, and should be entitled to privileged status under the law. They also indicate that they believe this individual should not accept gifts from news sources, nor should he seek social intimacy with these sources.

Type 3 individuals (n=4) differ from the first two types in that they see no reasons why the ideal journalist should not accept services from his news sources or avoid social contact with them. They also indicate that he should be self confident and see his job as interesting and respectable. He should feel free to withhold information he feels is detrimental to the public welfare but should also feel free to emphasize the sensational aspects of the events he covers in order to attract the attention of his audience, even to the point of shocking his audience occasionally.

These individuals also agree that the ideal journalist should not be arrogant or unethical nor should he view his job as merely a route to power, but he should not go so far as to think of the job as a chance to inform society regardless of the personal reward involved or attempt to advance the welfare of society instead of his own.

In short Type 3 individuals are more willing to acknowledge the material rewards of a career in journalism and to accept this as an important part of the job.

Type 4 individuals (n = 9) are much more traditional in their perception of the ideal journalist. They believe that he should be basically honest and should see his job as interesting and respectable, but that he should have no more rights than the average citizen. He may emphasize his point of view when reporting controversial material but should report all sides equally. He must adhere to the morals of his society and should refuse anything of value from a news source. If he makes social contact with a news source it should be in an official capacity only. Finally he should look on a career in journalism as a chance to advance the welfare of society and not himself and certainly not as a route to power.

Type 5 individuals (n = 6) have quite a different perception of the ideal journalist. They strongly agree that he should have extra legal protection so as to insure full information to his audience. However, they also feel that he should make every effort to counter his own views by seeking opposing views on the subject and should avoid forming opinions on controversial matters.

These individuals also agree that the primary goal of the ideal journalist should be to advance the welfare of society and not himself and should view the profession as a chance to inform society, not as a means of gaining personal reward or power.

Finally they agree that he may accept gifts from his news source if there are no strings attached.

At the opposite end of the scale this type feels that the ideal journalist should not be attracted to the job by the excitement or glamour nor should he attempt to shock his audience regardless of the consequences. They also indicate that while he should not be arrogant he should not attempt to be inconspicuous either. Finally they strongly disagree with the ideal that the journalist should be licensed by the government.

While it is evident from the foregoing that the respondents feel that the ideal journalist should hold many of the traditional qualities espoused by the journalistic code of ethics the question remains to be answered; how do they perceive the journalist as he actually exists today? What are the major areas of difference between the "ideal" journalist and the "real" journalist in the eyes of these high school students?

THE 'REAL' JOURNALIST

Analysis of the data pertaining to their perception of the "real" journalist indicates some major deviations between their ideal and the real.

Five types of individuals can be identified on the basis of their responses to the 40 statements concerning their perception of the ethics of the practicing journalist. The only point on which all 37 respondents agree when evaluating the journalist is that he has a set of ethical standards which are indeed higher than others in his society. However, they differ markedly over some facets of his ethics.

Type 1 (n = 24) is the largest group of individuals. They feel that the practicing journalist does indeed see his job as interesting and respectable and displays a degree of self confidence that is essential to his role in society. They also feel that he works to advance the welfare of society, even to the extent that he foregoes personal reward in doing so. They feel he has extra legal protection to insure full information to his public, but is also willing to cooperate with officials when asked to withhold information which may be detrimental to the public welfare.

They also feel that the journalist is basically honest and tends to emphasize his own point of view but counters it by seeking opposing views so that he can report all sides of any question equally. They also feel that he finds social contacts with news sources useful and that he will accept gifts from his news sources. However, in spite of this generally favorable view these individuals also tend to feel that the practicing journalist views his job as a route to power and prestige and often tries to shock his audience regardless of the consequences of such reporting.

Type 2 (n = 6) also hold a relatively favorable view of the practicing journalist but have some criticism not evident in Type 1 responses. For example these individuals feel that the journalist is pushy and opinionated; he tends to emphasize the sensational and to promote his own point of view. He will accept gifts from his news sources if "there are no strings attached," and finds social contact with his news sources "useful." To this group the journalist does not have higher ethical standards than others in his society.

Type 3 (n = 3) perceive the practicing journalist as being more of an advocate than an objective reporter. They feel he tends to promote his own point of view and to withhold information which he feels is detrimental to the public welfare. He sees his job as a chance to advance the welfare of society over himself and makes use of social contacts with his news sources in both an official and an unofficial capacity. They feel he has a privileged status under the law and has extra legal protection. On the other hand they do not believe that he is licensed by the government or that he willingly accepts gifts from his news sources.

Type 4 (n = 1) is the lone purist in the group. This individual believes the practicing journalist to be humble, honest and willing to report all sides of an event equally. He is not pushy, attracted to the job by the excitement or glamour and is subject to normal ethical restraints. He does not look at his job as a route to power or prestige.

Type 5 (n = 3) includes individuals who see the journalist as an individual licensed by the government and one who cooperates with officials to withhold information of a detrimental nature. All of his social contacts with news sources are of an official nature. He is not unethical and does not promote his own point of view, nor does he accept favors from his news sources. He is not subject to strict accountability nor does he tend to emphasize the sensational as a means of attracting his audience, or attempt to shock them. In short he functions as a happy public official.

Conclusions

The study in no way solves the problem of who the "journalist" is. He will very likely remain a mixture, in infinitely various proportions, of the WoodwardBernsteinJohnsonHearst ingredients. What the study does, we believe, is to point to a method of measuring something too frequently regarded as not subject to measurement. True, there is no information in this pilot study which could more sharply define the relationship between attitudes and the models or images on which these attitudes are based. That is a solvable problem, and the ongoing revision of the instrument seeks that information as well as the clarification of some statements themselves. Its further administration to different populations, in university journalism and non-journalism programs, to practicing journalists and the public, may well yield a pattern of attitude formation and change that can lead to definition of other influences.

What does strike the authors is a "confirmation," however slight, of the folk wisdom which holds that aspiring journalists are idealists, not totally in the mold of their elders but striving to correct some of the "errors" that they see. That recognition is necessary to those who have, in the words of Professor George Gordon, "the obligation of all teachers of journalism to construct a viable moral substructure for the young men and women who are preparing to pursue this well established profession tomorrow . . ." [2] That sounds like journalism "buff" Robert Redford, who reportedly became interested in Watergate after overhearing reporters discussing the affair and declaring that no newsman would ever pursue, let alone uncover, the full story. According to *Time:* "Redford was shocked: 'I've always had a very low regard for cynicism; I think it is the beginning of dying.' " [3] Redford, in his attempt to portray Bob Woodward in "All the President's Men", might become an ethical model for idealistic young journalists. What this study is seeking perhaps is a tool with which to measure idealism, or its antithesis. In conscientious hands it could be a tool with which to fight cynicism, a terminal condition for responsible journalism.

Footnotes

1. R.G. Collingwood, **The Idea of History** (New York: Oxford University Press) 1956, p. 3.
2. George N. Gordon in John C. Merrill and Ralph D. Barney (eds.), **Ethics and the Press** (New York: Hastings House) 1975, p. xiii.
3. "Watergate on Film," **Time,** March 29, 1975, p. 55.

As part of its service to the state's mass media, the Journalism Research Center will prepare and distribute occasionally a series of reports relating to journalism in Oklahoma. Material appearing in *Oklahoma Journalism Reports* may be reproduced freely. However, we request that the source be acknowledged and that a copy of the publication be sent to the Journalism Research Center. If you would like extra copies of this or any other issues of the *Oklahoma Journalism Reports* series to distribute to your staff or for any other purposes, reprints may be purchased at cost. We invite your comments and suggestions regarding topics for future reports. Please direct queries and comments to Dr. Gerald L. Grotta, Research Coordinator, at AC 405, 325-4181, or to Dr. Bob Carrell, Director, AC 405, 325-2721.

PART II
Writing Basics and Copy Formats

Exercise 10 Getting the reader's attention *(Chapter 4)*

If the lead fails, the story fails. You must provide enough information up front to attract and interest the readers and draw them into the story. This is no less true of routine stories than of the "big" stories. From the information below, write the following leads:

1. A summary lead.
2. A rewrite of the first lead, still summary style.
3. A question lead.
4. A "background" lead.

Reporter's notes:

Strike of building trades workers in three Cleveland County unions started two weeks ago today. Involved are 700 members of United Plumbers Guild Local 235; 1,500 members of Affiliated Hod Carriers of America Local 395; 900 members of Sheet Metal Workers Assn. of America Local 75. The plumbers demand a 45-cent-an-hour increase immediately, 15 cents an hour more a year from the date of the contract and 15 cents more an hour a year after that. The sheet metal workers want 50 cents an hour now, 15 cents an hour in a year and 10 cents an hour in two years. The hod carriers want 60 cents an hour now with a chance to reopen negotiations in two years. All three of the contracts expired two weeks ago. Negotiations with the employers, Associated Contractors Inc., had broken down a week earlier. The contractors offered 20 cents an hour over the next three years, 10 cents now. Picket lines were set up this week around three construction sites in Norman. The unions' headquarters have been established in the Trade Union Building. No violence has been reported. All construction activity in the county has been halted. No negotiations are scheduled.

Exercise 11 Leads for the ear
(Chapter 4)

From the notes in Exercise 10, write two different leads for the strike story in broadcast style. It helps to think of a broadcast lead as a single major point, perhaps expressed in two sentences, rather than a single long sentence.

Grade or Score_____ Name/Date_____

Exercise 12 From print to broadcast *(Chapter 4)*

From the following newspaper-style leads, rewrite, in *two* sentences, leads in broadcast style.

1. A new draft report being prepared by the Senate Intelligence Committee on the Iran arms-Contra affair says one of the president's chief motivations in approving the arms transfer was the release of U. S. hostages in Lebanon, congressional sources said today.

2. Troops were placed on "red alert" in Manila on Monday as thousands of people prepared to march on the presidential palace to protest last week's killing by soldiers of 12 demonstrators, according to officials of Bayan, the nation's largest leftist organization.

3. President Reagan is expected to talk about catastrophic health insurance in his State of the Union speech Tuesday night for the second straight year, but, once again, what he will say remains a mystery even to government health officials.

4. The second International Advisory Council Leadership Seminar, designed to solve problems facing international student leaders, accomplished its goal, seminar coordinator Marge Pryately said.

5. Police took black activist Winnie Mandela and her daughter from their home in the township of Soweto, near Johannesburg, Monday after confiscating some documents, but a police spokesman in Pretoria said Mandela was not formally in custody.

EXERCISE 12 / 29

Exercise 13 Under the umbrella

(Chapter 4)

The "umbrella" lead, constructed of the common elements in several separate stories, effectively covers and ties together a news package.

From the leads in Exercise 12, write *two* different umbrella leads for stories 1 and 3, and *two* umbrella leads for stories 2 and 5.

Exercise 14 Building a story

(Chapter 5)

Facts don't tell themselves; they must be organized for the reader or listener. Build a straightforward but complete story from the notes below.

Traffic fatality: 500 N. Miller Ave. (near downtown) in River City
Time: 3:00 a.m.
Victim: Carla Jo Longhorn, 25, of Bethany (dead at scene)
Injured: Marilyn Bourlier, 25, of River City
Sherrill Jo Martin, 21, of River City
Condition: Bourlier, satisfactory, in River City Memorial Hospital
Martin, treated for bruises and released
Circumstances: Bourlier was driver, Martin was front-seat passenger, Longhorn was backseat passenger. Car, southbound on Miller at high rate of speed, went out of control, crossed residential lawn and hit a tree. All occupants ejected.
Investigating officer: Corporal Paul Swenson, River City PD

Exercise 15 Quoting the source   (Chapter 5)

Direct quotations can add both information and "flavor" to a story and enhance credibility. Employ them where practical in the following two stories.

1. Notes from Cleveland County Sheriff's incident log:

   Residential burglary reported by telephone at 1900, 4 February, at 2456 120th Ave. NE. Reporting party: James Lewis Barnard. RP came home, found front door kicked in, called sheriff immediately. Items missing include 2 color televisions, 1 VCR, 1 microwave oven, 2 shotguns, 2 handguns, jewelry worth $5,000 and about $100 cash. Neighbor, R.L. Waddle, 2450 120th NE, saw white old-model pickup truck near Barnard's garage about noon; it was gone when he looked again at 1400.

   Interview notes from Deputy Marvin Barnes:

   Seventh burglary this month in northeast part of county. Always similar items taken. A pickup truck seen near three previous burglaries; no people spotted. "The sheriff is concerned because neighborhood residents are talking about armed citizen patrols during daylight hours."

   Notes from phone conversation with J.L. Barnard:

   "I'm cleaned out. This is the third time in two years. The sheriff ain't doing his job. We're going to blow someone away if they don't stay away from our homes. Everybody out here is mad as hell."

2. Notes from news conference at Hamilton Regional Hospital:

   Presentation by hospital administrator Jim Jones. Hospital is beginning fund drive to equip nuclear medicine treatment facility. Will be first in state outside of teaching hospitals. Projected cost is $3,500,000. Drive will run for one year from first of next month. Federal grant money from National Institutes of Health will supply $1,000,000 if drive can raise $2,500,000. Availability of facility would draw top doctors and researchers to Hamilton, according to a study done a year ago by the state department of health.

   Presentation by Mrs. Clarice Hensley, president of hospital auxiliary:

   Campaign will be run strictly by volunteers; no overhead except for printing and postage for mass mailings. Volunteers can sign up at hospital any time. "There will be a speaker's bureau with doctors, civic leaders and famous scientists available to civic groups on request. Hamilton is well known for its progressive community spirit. We are confident of success."

Grade or Score_____ Name/Date_____

Exercise 16 More notes and quotes (Chapter 5)

Both of the following stories rely to some extent on statements from parties involved. From each set of notes, write a story no longer than one page, playing the appropriate quotations prominently.

1. Telephone notes from conversation with fire dispatcher:

   Citizen phoned in report of fire at 5:39 a.m. today at the Budget Food Market at 24th and Alameda in Fairfield. Station 1 dispatched Truck 1, Ladder 1, Engines 1 and 11 and Unit 601 (Assistant Chief Jon Rice). Units arrived on scene at 5:42, and Rice radioed a second alarm. Truck 3, Engine 3 and Utility 33 dispatched from Station 3 and Chief Roy Sanders was called from home. Second alarm units cleared scene at 9:01 a.m.; all first alarm units except Engine 1 cleared by noon.

   Telephone notes from conversation with Chief Sanders:

   Store was fully involved when first units arrived. Second alarm was called mainly for manpower. "The fire was stubborn, particularly in the ceiling area. Contents are a total loss, primarily from smoke and water damage. We'll have to have an architectural survey to see if the building is still structurally sound. We're concerned about the cause. It looks peculiar, but we haven't found a definite ignition source." Damage estimate is pending; store owned by Budget Markets Inc.; of Omaha, NE.

2. Reporter's notes from press conference held by Howard K. Smith, president of East Fairfield Citizen Action Committee, held last night at ThunderFun Cafe at 108th NE and Alameda, Norman:

   The committee, formed in the past week, is to promote public safety in the east Fairfield area. Area is semi-rural, isolated homes, lot of traffic, particularly on spring and summer weekends with traffic to Lake Thunderbird. Dangers are burglarly ("a rash in recent months"), gunshots from unauthorized hunters ("I've got bullet holes in my barn"), vandalism and litter from lake visitors, fires set by campers and drunk driving. "We want planning and some help from the sheriff, some solutions to our problems. If we don't get it, we'll take care of ourselves." Group will organize patrols with citizens' band radios and rifles or shotguns. Hours aren't fixed yet. Meeting serves in part as public warning to criminals and warning to sheriff to act or be removed.

   Phone notes from conversation with Sheriff J.C. Kennedy:

   "We recognize the problem and are doing the best we can with our resources. We discourage armed patrols. They're dangerous. I hope they're careful. We'll meet any time, any place."

Grade or Score_____ Name/Date_____

Exercise 17 Facts and figures   (Chapter 5)

Numbers (dollars, quantities, statistics) are difficult to handle clearly and without disrupting the flow of a story, yet they are often the point of the story. In the following stories, use the ones you need, but don't overburden the story line.

From each set of notes, develop a story of no more than two-thirds of a page.

1. Telephone notes from City Hall reporter:

   City Controller Gerald Carson said he thought the city would bring in $9,642,800 from sales taxes this year, but it now appears the take will only be $9,256,800. He says sales tax collections have been going down for four months. Also, only 35% of building permits to date have been collected. Other licenses and permits are down. Carson's letter detailing the shortfalls says they will amount to around $100,000. The city may save $100,000 or more because of rebates from Blue Cross-Blue Shield premiums from the past year. Carson did the revenue and expense updating after it was requested by the acting city manager. Dave Clark is acting city manager. The estimates for this year which were off were based on projections from the utility rate increase which the voters passed in December. City officials thought the collections would come in for five months in the fiscal year, but it turns out to be only four months. So after the present and following fiscal years, the city will be short approximately $1,000,000.

2. Reporter's notes from interview with Dr. Donald Kassebaum, executive dean of state College of Medicine:

   Number of applicants for medical schools around United States is down 23% in last 10 years. There are 45% fewer applicants to the state college from within the state in the same time. In fall 1987, 142 students were admitted. The class could have held 176. 28 of the 142 were turned down once because of low test scores. The admissions board eventually let them in. K. says it was political pressure. The college budget was reduced $900,000 last year because of the number of students admitted. When class size is reduced, funding is reduced. K. says the college is trying for 150 students for next fall. No more than 20% of students admitted can be from out of state. K. says 13 of the 28 students first turned down have had academic problems. He says the college won't pass students if they don't meet academic standards.

Grade or Score_____ Name/Date_____

Exercise 18 Facts and figures out loud (Chapter 5)

If numbers are a problem in print, they are twice as much trouble in broadcast style. The solutions are, in part, elimination where possible and approximation were appropriate.

From the notes in Exercise 17, write each story in broadcast style, each about 30 seconds long.

Exercise 19 Quotes on the air (Chapter 5)

The trouble with quotation marks is that you can't hear them. As a consequence, most broadcast writers prefer to paraphrase statements rather than struggle with aural clues that will tell listeners they're hearing a direct quote rather than the announcer's wording. Sometimes, however, direct quotes are important to the mood or meaning of a story. They must be used judiciously and clearly set apart from the rest of the copy.

Work at least one direct quote from each of the speakers into the following story. These are not taped "sound bites"; they must be read by the announcer.

The story:

Major State University is embroiled in a controversy over dealings involving a race track. MSU is leasing land, through a third party, to the track developers. In brief, MSU leases land on a long-term, low-cost arrangement to the city zoo; the zoo builds and leases to MSU an animal research laboratory; the zoo leases the university's land and some of its own to the developer.

The words of the principal parties:

1. Stan Stanley, MSU chief legal counsel:

   "We could have negotiated for a 'piece of the action,' taking our money as a percentage of track income, but we decided not to be involved in the race-track proceeds. Our deal is structured strictly with the zoological society. We figured we would get a lot of criticism for even being a part of the racing question, and we thought this was the easiest way to get what we want without being involved in the so-called moral question of betting and all that."

2. Tony Jarvis, spokesman for Davis Developers:

   "We don't have to deal with the university directly. Our negotiations have been pleasant, if somewhat distant. Of course, MSU could have made a bundle of money under another arrangement, but they have their own fish to fry, and we are certainly just as happy not to have a bigger cut out of our potential income. Whatever they want is fine with us."

3. Penelope Dogood, president of the Anti-Vice League:

   "It is disgraceful that the university has chosen to associate itself with organized crime and all the other unsavory people who are involved in gambling and taking money from the poor. Times may be hard for everyone, but MSU cannot afford to give up its position of moral leadership for the sake of mere money. Students and faculty are surely willing to give up some frills to avoid the odious imputation that they are profiting from someone else's misery. MSU President Smith, as a good Christian, should never have allowed the university to sink so low."

Grade or Score_____ Name/Date_____

Exercise 20 Writing to audiotape   (Chapter 5)

Using radio effectively means letting the audience hear for themselves—that is, hear the sounds and voices of the story rather than an announcer's description. Good editing can shorten, simplify and enhance a taped interview, integrating it into a script, which sets up the "sound bites" with identification of the speaker but doesn't give away the substance of the bite.

From the following information and transcript of an interview, write two "packages," one of 45 seconds total length and one of 1 minute 15 seconds. For ease of timing, the interview transcript lines are about 60 characters, or four seconds long.

The situation:

You have just taped an interview with Mayor Tim Johnson following a news conference in which he announced severe budget cuts for city services. Total reductions in the $146,000,000 budget amount to $13,450,000. The police department will lose 12% of its patrol force and special units for juveniles and sex crimes. The fire department will close one station (on the far east side at 72nd and Alameda streets) and trim one man from its three-men-per-truck teams. Rumors of the cuts have been around for days, and a group of east side residents has filed a petition asking for a grand jury investigation of city finances.

The interview (R = reporter, J = Johnson):

R: What's the cause of this 15% cut in the budget?
J: Well . . . it's not really 15%, more like 9 or 10.
R: Whatever it is, what's the problem?
J: Not enough money coming in.
R: From where?
J: The usual sources of city revenue: utility charges and sales taxes . . . the hotel-motel tax is way down, too, but the city doesn't get that money directly for government expenses. It goes to arts and tourist promotion and things like that. I guess it's just the economy in general, and of course we won't be getting any more of that good federal matching money which was at least 10 or 11 million last year.
R: Couldn't the city officials see this coming?
J: Apparently not.
R: How badly will this hurt the citizens?
J: Well . . . they aren't going to like having fewer cops on the street, and I don't know what will happen to the crime rate. That always gets people upset. The fire department is in trouble too, but Chief Davis tells me his people will just do the best they can.
R: Speaking of the fire department, why was the decision made to cut station 6 out on Alameda, after all the fight about getting one out there a few years ago? Surely somebody expected the east siders to get mad about that.
J: Somebody always gets mad. The department said that one makes the fewest runs, so it seemed all right to me.
R: But statistics used at the time of the fight showed that the dollar loss per fire out there was greater than any other fires because of the long response time.
J: Maybe the chief thought better a few big fires than a lot of small ones.

R: I don't understand.
J: I mean . . . maybe it's better to have a bigger loss in a few fires than to have a bunch of small ones that get bigger . . . or something like that. Ask Davis, that's his thing.
R: You didn't say anything about new taxes or other ways to raise money.
J: Well . . . of course we'll study the problem. Of course, if business is down, then the sales taxes are going to stay down, unless we raise the rate of tax, and I don't think people would be too crazy about that. The state can't help and the feds can't help. Maybe the best thing would be a group of citizens to come up with a proposal or proposals that could provide some money.
R: I didn't notice anything in your statement about cutting some other city services like garbage collection or going up on the rates for water and sewer. Have you considered these?
J: I'm sure the council members and the city staff have looked at these options and just didn't think that was the way to solve the problem.
R: Won't this appear to be what some people have already called a plan to scare folks into voting for more taxes because they're worried about fire and police protection, when it could have been solved another way?
J: I don't care what some people think. They're not doing anything to solve the problem. We're doing the best we can.
R: People on the east side don't think so, apparently. Does the grand jury petition bother you? Is there any basis for the complaints?
J: The east side always complains. They complain about everything we do for them. All they're doing is getting in the way.
R: When will this emergency be over?
J: I guess when people realize we need more money . . . maybe taxes, maybe less service, maybe some bright idea. It could go on a long time.

Exercise 21 ... And more writing to audiotape (Chapter 5)

Audiotape is a good way to get both sides of a dispute into one story, each side in its own words. The trick is to make sure the presentation is balanced. In the following story, use at least one "bite" from each person in each of two packages, one 45 seconds long and the other 1 minute 30 seconds.

The situation:

A $25 million job retraining bill is now under consideration in the state legislature. As proposed, first priority for financial aid for retraining would go to out-of-work oil field employees. Up to 80 percent of the money would go to this category, with all others lumped into the remaining 20 percent. Naturally the "oilies" are opposed by the farm bloc, which insists its constituency should have first priority. You have interviews with the two principal spokespersons: Representative Lonnie Green, majority leader in the house, who backs the oil workers; and Representative Hester Adams, minority whip in the house, who backs the farmers.

The interviews (R = Reporter, G = Green, A = Adams):

R: Why should oil workers have the bulk of the benefits?
G: Unemployment runs highest, percentagewise, in the oil industry, so we should be putting as many of these people as possible back to work. The state needs the money we'll get from their taxes; they ain't doing much for us right now.
R: Don't we need the farmers' money in taxes?
G: There's plenty of farms to be worked. They can find jobs. They been getting government aid for years. It didn't work. My priorities are right. We need to put the money where the need is.
R: Some opponents have said we shouldn't be retraining workers who will go back to the oil patch when the industry improves.
G: Why not? Then they'll have something to fall back on if the Arabs decide to flood the market again. It's kinda like insurance.
R: What can these workers be trained to do?
G: Anything mechanical. We need welders, electricians, plumbers, car mechanics . . . people like that. When I think what it costs me to get my car fixed, I think we could use more competition in that business. Same with the plumbing in my house.
R: Are you optimistic that the bill will pass as written?
G: It's what the majority wants.
R: Majority of the legislature or majority of the people?
G: Same thing.

R: Are farmers getting a fair shake?
A: Of course not. Big industry is making a play for the taxpayers' money to take the load off their backs, and we won't stand for it. Farmers have made this country what it is, and now we've got to help them.
R: Will people really leave the farm to be retrained?
A: Too many times they don't have a choice. The banks and the tax people are taking away the farms, and these people aren't going to go on welfare. They want jobs. They've been here longer than the oil field people, and we owe them more. These "oilies" are transient. We don't have any responsibility for them.

R: What kind of training is appropriate for ex-farmers?
A: Almost anything. These people have been private entrepreneurs, and they could learn any trade.
R: What happens to the farm economy if too many farmers take up this training?
A: Only those who can't make it on the farm would do this. They love farming too much to give it up if they can even break even.
R: What are the chances of getting the bill changed?
A: Big-business forces are lined up against us, but the good sense of the people will prevail. Their voice will be heard over the clamor of self-interest in the capitol. People of the soil will triumph.

Grade or Score_____ Name/Date_____

Exercise 22 Words and pictures *(Chapter 5)*

The key to writing for television news film or tape is learning when *not* to write. Let pictures speak for themselves wherever possible. Describe what is not in a particular scene, not what *is* in it.

In this exercise, the tape is edited with the scene length and scene order indicated. Fit the relevant information from the general notes to the visual story. This is strictly a voice-over, not a stand-up, and requires no introduction or tagline.

Reporter's notes from the scene:

Semi-trailer gasoline tanker truck overturned this morning at 8:30, in the middle of rush hour traffic, on Interstate 40 near the interchange with Interstate 35. Truck braked hard to avoid a swerving car, jackknifed and rolled on its side across three lanes of traffic. Two autos hit the truck from behind but sustained only minor damage. Truck leaked what firemen estimate was 5,000 gallons of gasoline onto Interstate 40. Traffic is still being detoured three miles around the site on secondary roads. Highway patrol says it will be two more hours before traffic is clear. Driver of truck: John S. Murphy, 36, Little Rock, Ark., employed by Johnson Transports of Little Rock. Murphy is at Baptist Hospital being treated for minor injuries. Traffic was backed up at one time for four miles. Police say three other minor accidents resulted from "sightseers." There was no fire. Investigation is continuing, but driver likely will not be cited.

Shot breakdown:

1. Wide shot—five seconds—patrol car and trooper in foreground, big pool of dark liquid on road, tanker in middle background, cars in far background passing on other side of highway.
2. Medium shot—four seconds—from front of truck, low angle, two fire trucks in background with hoses playing on gas pool.
3. Closeup—two seconds—two firemen handling hose near nozzle.
4. Medium closeup—three seconds—two highway patrolmen conferring, truck in background.
5. Medium wide shot—four seconds—highway patrol car, lights flashing, near barricade, patrolman waving traffic off to access road.
6. Wide shot—four seconds—long lines of cars, moving slowly, edging into one lane.
7. Medium shot—five seconds—wrecker pulling to stop near cab of semi-trailer and backing.
8. Wide shot—five seconds—from back up the road behind traffic being detoured, tanker visible in distant background.

Grade or Score_____ Name/Date_____

Exercise 23 Pictures and words (Chapter 5)

The second television script is generally easier than the first. Just remember: Don't write if you don't have to.

Reporter's notes from the scene:

House fire reported this morning in south River City, 4234 S. Walker, at 5:30. Engine 25, Truck 25, Rescue 2 and District Chief 5 responded. On arrival, first engine found two-bedroom frame house with heavy smoke coming from all doors and windows. No visible flames. A half-dozen neighbors were standing in the front yard. Firemen entering the house were first driven back by flames in front room and hall; knocked down flames with first hose line. Other firemen entered rear door. Found a woman and two children unconscious on separate beds in two rooms and carried them outside. All three transported to South Community Hospital by Amcare ambulances. Fire suppressed and declared out at 6:10 a.m. During final search and cleanup, firemen found body of child under bed in one room previously searched. Resuscitation failed and child pronounced dead at scene. Police and medical examiner called to scene. Fire Marshal E.W. Koch said, after initial investigation, that fire origin is not clear and will be investigated as suspicious because of fatality. Damage to house estimated by District Chief Bill Krause at $12,000. Hospital says all three victims are in serious condition: Debra Humphrey, 29, of the house address; Lisa Humphrey, 9, same address; Bobby Humphrey, 6, same address. Dead child identified tentatively by neighbors as Lynn Humphrey, about 4, same address. Medical examiner's report pending.

Shot breakdown:

1. Wide shot—five seconds—police tape line in foreground, house in background, officers standing in yard.
2. Medium shot—three seconds—firemen standing in street near truck, looking at house.
3. Medium wide shot—six seconds—ambulance attendants carrying stretcher out front door and across lawn, past camera and out of frame.
4. Medium shot—five seconds—ambulance attendants load stretcher and close door.
5. Medium shot—four seconds—police and firemen conferring over notes with front of house in background.
6. Closeup—two seconds—police detective taking notes.
7. Closeup—two seconds—fire chief nodding at detective.
8. Wide shot—four seconds—police car in foreground, lights flashing, house in background.

Grade or Score_____   Name/Date_____

Exercise 24 Writing for videotex and teletext   *(Chapter 6)*

Your paper's videotex service would likely provide local stories in two forms: a brief form for the "browser" and a more complete account for those who want all the details. Write both from the following notes.

Fire this morning at Central Mid-High School, located in 200 block of North Ponca Avenue. Discovered about 6:30 a.m. by janitor William Henry, 56, who called the fire department. Fire destroyed all contents and records in two offices. It gutted the two offices and the foyer of the school. Records destroyed included student grades, attendance records and disciplinary records. Smoke damaged four classrooms. Only the janitor was in the building when the fire started. He suffered second- and third-degree burns on his hands and arms while trying to put out the fire. Hospitalized at Mercy Hospital. Four fire trucks responded and the fire was put out in about 30 minutes. Fire Inspector Neil Roberts said there are definite signs of an incendiary device. Pieces of a Molotov cocktail were discovered, and there was a strong smell of gasoline at the scene. Fire officials are seeking information from anyone who might have noticed any suspicious activity near the school this morning. Principal Dale Ernst says several classes have been moved because of the damage, some to the new gymnasium and one to the cafeteria. Charles Bumgarner, assistant superintendent for facilities, placed the damage estimate at about $100,000. Four hundred students attend the school.

Exercise 25 More videotex   (Chapter 6)

Do two versions of this story, as in Exercise 24.

Two-fatality accident, 11 a.m. today, at intersection of Elm and Lindsey at the corner of the Major State University campus. Two girls were killed. Both were MSU students. They were standing on the sidewalk at the corner, apparently on their way to class. A yellow sports car jumped the curb and struck both girls. They died instantly. Identification of victims: Lynn Pebbles, 18, freshman from Boston, and Bettie Allen, 18, freshman from Tulsa. Both were MSU cheerleaders. Identification of driver: George Rhoades, 23, sociology graduate student from Dallas, driving a 1972 Porsche. Rhoades is in Mercy Hospital with broken jaw, broken nose and numerous cuts and bruises. A passenger in his car, Tina Merrill, 21, of New York City, was not injured. Investigating officer Sgt. J.W. Carmichael says evidence indicates Rhoades was speeding and driving recklessly. He says Rhoades told him he was hurrying because he was late for a class. Fifteen students are listed as eyewitnesses. Carmichael says he will talk to the district attorney about the possibility of manslaughter charges. Funeral arrangements for the two girls are pending.

Exercise 26 The interview *(Chapter 7)*

Successful interviewing is much more than asking the right questions; it depends on careful listening. A pause in place of a quick question may elicit additional comment from the interviewee, something spontaneous that could be more important or interesting than an answer to a question. Interview a fellow student about his or her career goals, being sure to listen carefully, picking up clues for follow-up questions. Keep your attention on the *person,* not the story.

Grade or Score_____ Name/Date_____

Exercise 27 Multiple interviews for a single story *(Chapter 7)*

Interview a minimum of four fellow students for a wrap-up story on knowledge of and attitudes toward either (1) the Strategic Defense Initiative ("Star Wars") or (2) acquired immune deficiency syndrome (AIDS). Remember, if the questions are not consistent from interview to interview, you won't have any basis for the comparison of answers.

Comparing and contrasting the views expressed, write a story of no more than one and one-half pages with a summary lead and at least one direct quotation from each interviewee.

Grade or Score_____ Name/Date_____

Exercise 28 Combining quotes for broadcast (Chapter 7)

Using multiple interviews in broadcast copy, without audiotape, requires considerable care with respect to identification of the interviewee. Rewrite the preceding exercise as a one-minute broadcast story, using at least one brief direct quote from each interviewee.

Exercise 29 Reporting speeches *(Chapter 8)*

Most speeches can be improved in the process of reporting them, if only because the report is generally shorter than the speech. Some speeches, on the other hand, can lose much of their impact or even their major points because the report is unduly brief or appropriate quotes aren't used.

From the following (edited) transcript of a speech by Peter Jennings of ABC News to a convention of the Radio-Television News Directors Association, write a story emphasizing his major thesis. Rely heavily on his actual words, using a minimum of connecting narrative.

Today we put words and pictures through the air, but generals still don't like reporters on the battlefield and politicians still complain bitterly about coverage of them.

As to responsibility and bias, I hope you will agree with me that we have, for the most part, emerged from adolescence to adulthood. And I am sure you will agree with me that we remain one of the most talked about institutions in modern society.

Today, a major story, as reported on television, is likely to go through three very predictable stages. The reporting of the story itself. Then the "media press" reporting on how we reported the story, and then our recriminations about their reporting on us.

In some respects, I think this is all very healthy, though perhaps too self-absorbed or too self-centered for much of the audience. I think that recent criticism has led to a more thoughtful dialogue between us and the public, and I think it has led to a marginal improvement in the way we do our jobs.

It pays us never to forget that we live in a consumer society where people expect to be heard if they have a complaint about the product.

I think we all understand now that the media agenda is not accepted by all the people all the time, but every study shows us we do play a significant role in ordering the priorities. When we allow a story such as the TWA ordeal to so dominate our thinking, we miss other priorities.

During that period, the House passed a bill to restart testing for chemical and biological warfare, thus ending President Nixon's moratorium of 15 years ago, *without* the opportunity that we provide for public debate. We suddenly took the focus off tax reform, and a great many legislators will tell you that broke its back.

We also left people up in the air on the subject of wasteful spending at the Pentagon. Oh, yes, we'll get back to it, but suddenly one day it was a big issue, and the next it was not. There is nothing like a crisis to test our critical judgments on the universe. I think a lot of the viewers who rely on us feel cheated in those circumstances.

We do tend to run and hide a little in the face of criticism. My only suggestion for next time would be that we query our critics on whether they have seen what we really do. Much of the criticism is based on such flimsy evidence that I suspect it is often based on reading about what we do rather than having actually watched us.

There is certainly an up side to what I have to say. It is very healthy to find so many competing voices in the media, including conservative voices. I am more than ever convinced that whatever our private political views, the great majority of us check our more obvious prejudices at the door. While I agree that *all reporting,* by definition, is editorializing, in the sense that it requires choice, I would direct our more fervent critics to innumerable studies on bias in the evening news.

It is not ideology which concerns me about our reporting. It is perspective and context. I think both are in short supply, often in the way we see ourselves as communities and certainly in the way we see America as part of the whole world. I either disagree with Marshall McLuhan or I never understood him. Television is not a message unto itself. It is a medium.

This does not mean we don't have, as I've suggested, extraordinary power. When we *convey the message,* the people trying to make policy and a massive public are affected simultaneously.

I think there is a reasonable chance that public confidence in us *will erode* if we do not keep our fellow citizens in touch with the world's realities, not just an administration's wishful thinking of what it should be.

We cannot lose sight of the fact that all over the world people who are illiterate have been enfranchised by television. In a world much smaller yet more complex than it was 40 years ago, television viewers in free, democratic societies should be informed and enlightened by it. Ed Murrow said that at this convention 30 years ago.

Our children now go around the world before they learn to cross the street. We know what happened in Cairo before we eat breakfast. Television has changed what we know and when we will know it.

Now if we can only improve our understanding as much as we've improved the pictures . . .

PART III
Complex Story Structures

Exercise 30 Covering the speech *(Chapter 8)*

Covering a speech takes a special kind of listening skill. Frequently, part of a major point will have slipped by before the reporter recognizes it, and the ability to recall how it was introduced is important. Equally important is finding the key element in a speech, which sometimes is not the one the speaker emphasizes. Take notes carefully, review them immediately after the speech and expand them as necessary while the memory is still fresh. Then, only then, can you begin to frame the story around the significant facts.

Cover a speech on campus or in some public meeting (but not a lecture; lectures are seldom constructed in the same fashion as a speech). Use a tape recorder if allowed; it helps with accurate direct quotes. Be sure you know something about the speaker. His or her words alone don't explain the significance of the remarks without credentials.

Do the story in two versions: a print story of a maximum of 300 words and a broadcast story of 45 seconds.

Exercise 31 After the speech

(Chapter 8)

A good speech frequently will prompt a desire for more information. On the basis of the speech you covered for Exercise 30, prepare a list of at least five specific questions you would ask in an interview for more detail in writing a more comprehensive story. With the questions, indicate which points or themes in the speech itself prompted the questions.

Grade or Score_____   Name/Date_____

Exercise 32 Covering meetings (Chapter 9)

Covering meetings in person is far preferable to relying on after-the-fact accounts by a participant. Aside from the obvious possibility of self-interest in the report of one who took part, there is no way for the reporter to catch the spirit and flavor of an interchange in debate, the reaction of the audience or the exact words of a "quotable" quote.

Cover a meeting that is convenient—student government or your faculty senate, for example. Be sure to obtain a copy of the agenda in advance; it not only allows you to anticipate controversial topics, it frequently helps to identify significant parties involved.

From your notes and observations, write a print story of no more than 300 words and a broadcast story of no more than 45 seconds.

Exercise 33 Not all meetings are alike (Chapter 9)

Often a reporter must cover a meeting at which he or she is somewhat "on the outside," having no substantial background in the subjects discussed. Such coverage demands some information beyond just what occurs in the meeting proper.

Cover a meeting of a city government group: council or commission, planning board, parks and recreation committee. Perhaps a civic club such as Kiwanis, Rotary, Lions or another has a program planned that sounds interesting. Besides taking notes of the meeting itself, talk to the parties involved so your reporting can be placed in context.

Write up your story as a print version of 250 words maximum and a broadcast version of no longer than 30 seconds.

Exercise 34 Public relations writing as a source (Chapter 10)

"Press releases" can be a source of information to the news media as well as a way of furthering the parochial interest of the group that issues one. Often they serve as the basis of feature stories or as public service announcements (PSAs) that put the newspaper or broadcast station behind some worthwhile effort.

Using the following release, write a brief print feature on the opportunities mentioned and a 20-second PSA for broadcast.

DEPARTMENT OF THE NAVY
NAVAL RESERVE CENTER
5316 S. DOUGLAS BLVD.
OKLAHOMA CITY, OKLAHOMA 73150-9702

NAVAL RESERVE
PUBLIC AFFAIRS

The U.S. Naval Reserve is looking for people with journalism, public relations, advertising, marketing or college teaching backgrounds to become reserve public affairs specialists.

Applicants are needed to fill paid positions as commissioned public affairs officers or as enlisted journalists. Officers and journalists qualify for pay billets, earn four days pay for each two-day monthly drill weekend and perform two weeks of active duty for training a year with active-duty Navy commands across the nation and overseas.

To qualify as a public affairs officer, applicants must have a baccalaureate degree in journalism, advertising or mass communications. If the degree is in another specialty, applicants should have experience in a journalism-related area. Prior military service is not a requirement. The maximum age limit for a commission is 35 years as of the date of appointment as an Ensign.

Naval Reserve public affairs officers drill monthly with public affairs units across the nation, including Office of Information Detachment 411 in Oklahoma City. Reservists train with other public affairs, newspaper, radio, television, marketing and media professionals; arrange news conferences for visiting Navy officials; respond to media inquiries during fast-breaking news events involving the Navy; write news and feature articles and produce radio and television productions for Navy and civilian markets; and maintain systematic news release programs through various media.

To qualify as an enlisted journalist, applicants should have experience in print media, radio, television and other journalism-related fields in civilian jobs such as a reporter, editor, announcer or producer. Journalist positions are available in advanced pay grades up to Petty Officer First Class with the opportunity to advance to Chief Journalist Petty Officer.

Officers and journalists develop and improve their professional qualifications through participation in a

Naval Reserve unit, enrollment in Navy correspondence courses, and participation in annual two-week training duty. In addition, officers and journalists build points toward a retirement pension in the Naval Reserve.

If you are interested in becoming a public affairs officer or journalist, please contact:

Lt. Cdr. Greg Slavonic 405-278-6077
Lt. Cdr. Ed Klecka 405-943-2406
Lt. Cdr. Bill Hickman 405-755-6902
Lt. Brian Marks 405-733-2926

# # #

Exercise 35 Public relations writing that gets attention

(Chapter 10)

Aside from an inherently interesting topic, one feature of a press release that will catch an editor's eye is a suggestion of something that his or her publication or station can do with the information that will individualize the coverage and create more public interest.

Write a press release of no more than one and a half double-spaced typed pages on an activity planned by an organization you belong to or that you're familiar with. Write it in a form that could be published as is, but include at the end (1) name and phone number of a person to contact for more information and (2) suggestions for picture and sound possibilities that would encourage newspaper photos or television visual treatment.

Grade or Score_____   Name/Date_____

Exercise 36 Promotion
(Chapter 10)

Every medium promotes itself. Newspapers call them house ads; radio and television stations call them promos. Whatever the term, it refers to a hybrid form between advertising and public relations.

Given the following information, create a 10-second and a 30-second promo for this hypothetical radio station. You might listen carefully to two or three local stations to confirm two basic rules of broadcast promotion: emphasis on dial position ("KJ-103") and a slogan ("More rock, less talk"), possibly accompanied by an "audio logo," a characteristic piece of music.

Station information:

Call letters: KSKS
Frequency: 108 MHz
Hours: 24 hours a day, seven days a week
Power: 3,000 watts (effective coverage about 20-mile radius from the city)
Format: Adult contemporary/non-network.
　　　　News—five minutes on the hour from 6 a.m. to midnight
Other: Aggressive promotion of local interest, stressing strong ties to your community

Grade or Score_____   Name/Date_____

Exercise 37 The "atmosphere" feature (Chapter 11)

The ability to paint word pictures is the feature writer's chief asset. It must be done subtly, by suggestion, not forcing the reader to some mental picture, but letting the reader fill in the outline the writer sketches.

Describe, in feature story form, your observance of some holiday: the Fourth of July, Thanksgiving, Memorial Day or a particular local holiday. Don't make it a "personal" account; keep it in the third person. Keep it short; feature writing doesn't mean license to ramble. Within one and a half double-spaced typewritten pages, suggest the "atmosphere" and "mood" of the observance along with the events, great or small, that characterized the day. In particular, search your memory for small but significant detail.

*Grade or Score*_____ *Name/Date*_____

Exercise 38 The personality feature *(Chapter 11)*

A perceptive journalist once described the business of journalism as "explaining people to people." An effective, but tricky, method is the personality profile. As with any feature, it requires subtlety, general descriptions rather than labels, hints rather than statements, and observations, not judgments.

Profile someone, other than a fellow student, who has caught your interest. It might be a family member, a favorite teacher, a boss or co-worker, a local "character." You can, perhaps should, interview that person, but don't use extensive quotes. Use significant physical description: appearance, clothing, movements, expressions.

Keep the length to one and a half double-spaced typewritten pages.

Grade or Score_____   Name/Date_____

Exercise 39 The whole versus the sum of its parts
(Chapter 11)

"Significant detail" is that which illuminates, characterizes or distinguishes a person, place, object or event from a mass of similar persons, places, objects and events. The selection of significant details can create a far more accurate picture than an attempt to craft a single descriptive phrase or statement.

   Visit a secondhand store, a pawn shop, a junkyard or an Army-Navy surplus store. Observe objects, people, physical characteristics of the scene. Then create a feature story of no more than one page that captures the atmosphere of the place. Use no quotes; if you need reference to conversation to complete the piece, characterize it by style, not by content.

Exercise 40 The feature on radio (Chapter 11)

Radio may be the ultimate easel for the feature writer–artist. Sounds are suggestive, not specific. They create what the radio writer calls "presence," the feeling of being at the scene, and they reinforce the words of the story without getting in the way. On occasion, the sounds actually carry the story, but only if they are easily identifiable or are introduced by the narration.

Take a scene familiar to almost everyone: shopping in a supermarket. Your assignment is to document the frantic pace in a checkout line at rush hour. In the body of the narration (script), indicate where and for how long you want certain sounds and whether the sounds should be "up full" (without narration over them) or "under" (with the announcer reading over them). It is a delicate balance.

Exercise 41 Every journalist a columnist *(Chapter 11)*

There has probably never been a journalist who didn't think that he or she was wise enough, clever enough and imaginative enough to be a columnist. Here is a chance to indulge a fantasy. In the process, you might see some similarities to feature writing. First, the subject must be interesting; clever writing won't brighten a dull topic. Second, *I* tends to be the longest word in the writing of most novice columnists. And third, just as in feature writing, subtlety or indirection is much more effective than pontification.

Your editor has allowed you to write a bylined column on any subject you want, within legal and ethical limits. You have one and a half double-spaced typewritten pages. And, the editor warns you, if you choose to be humorous (as do most beginning columnists), remember that senses of humor are as infinitely various as people.

Exercise 42 Depth reporting *(Chapter 12)*

Depth reporting requires careful investigation of multiple sources. Usually a good deal of material is in written form in laws, public records, books and magazines. Some of it must be gathered from participants or experts in a field. All must be woven together in simple, understandable fashion for the reader who cannot be assumed to have any prior knowledge of the subject. Perhaps most important, the subject must be presented in a way that excites reader interest. Why should he or she read something that doesn't immediately affect life or work? The writer's job is to show that effect up front in the story and make the reader care.

Your assignment is to explain "shield laws" to your readers. Aside from the obvious tasks of researching the history of shield laws generally, the status of legislation in your state and the varying opinions of practicing journalists and legal experts, you must convince the reader that the topic is important—to the reader, not just to other journalists.

Exercise 43 The depth of controversy (Chapter 12)

Depth stories are sometimes the best way to handle controversial topics. Along with the typical requirements of careful research to put the issues in perspective, the writer must strive for fairness, a more difficult condition than simple quantitative "balance."

For your depth story on the issue of a uniform national minimum drinking age, you need facts on the history of the proposal, the extent of compliance nationally, the status of legislation in your state and a wide, representative sample of opinion on the merits and drawbacks of such a law.

PART IV
Persuasive Writing

Exercise 44 Advertising: Selling an image *(Chapter 13)*

The situation:

You have a new product you must promote. It is a white table wine. It is, compared to existing wines on the market today, light, dry and elegant. It will be priced in the mid-range, neither inexpensive nor expensive. Your target market is defined as 25–35 years old, mostly single or young marrieds, living in urban areas, mostly college-educated and with a mean income of $30,000 annually. They are mostly young professional people with active professional and social lives. Your proposed ad will appear in a magazine directed to that market.

The assignment:

Name the wine. Visualize the personality or mood you wish to convey to the target market. Describe in writing the "look" you want to project to that market. Then write copy, including a headline, of not more than 80 words that gives form to the visualization.

Exercise 45 Advertising: Selling a style (Chapter 13)

The situation:

You are on the advertising sales staff of the local daily newspaper. One of your accounts is a new restaurant-club opening next week in an upscale semi-suburban area. It will have a specialized menu of "Tex-Mex" dishes, from the ordinary to the exotic. It features live music nightly (a mariachi band) from 8 p.m. to 1 a.m. There is a small dance floor. The restaurant is closed on Mondays. The bar can provide a full range of mixed drinks, but the specialty of the house is something the owner has quixotically named Montezuma's Revenge. The name of the new enterprise is Olé!, and its market target is singles and young marrieds, without children, well educated, who lead active professional and social lives. Their lifestyles embrace anything "international," from food to fashion.

The assignment:

Picture the personality and mood you want to convey to the target audience. Describe in writing the look you want. Then write a headline and copy, not to exceed 100 words, that carry through that style.

Grade or Score_____ Name/Date_____

Exercise 46 Advertising: Hearing the style *(Chapter 13)*

You, as a time salesperson (or "account executive," if you're paid enough) for the local radio station, have noticed the big campaign for Olé! in the local newspaper. You have all the information on the style and projected market for the restaurant (from Exercise 45), and you want a piece of the action.

The assignment:

Bearing in mind that your station's music format is MOR (middle of the road), put together a demonstration spot of 30 seconds, using an appropriate music bed, to play for the owner of Olé!. It should contain a slogan—short, unique and memorable.

Exercise 47 Reviews:
The journalist as interested observer *(Chapter 14)*

Reviews are meant for readers, not for producers, performers or, most important, for reviewers. When reviews become ego trips for the reviewer, they fail in their duty to advise the public on whether to spend time and money on a television show, play or book. Reviews should be informed by a body of knowledge about the field and controlled by a restraint on purely personal feelings of the reviewer. Everyone is a critic; reviewers simply have a larger audience, and they should treat it with respect.

With that in mind, write a one-page review of your favorite television show (of any type). Imagine that it is the first show of a season, and you must explain the series' theme and characters to your readers, as well as evaluating its strong and weak qualities.

Grade or Score_____ Name/Date_____

Exercise 48 Reviews:
The journalist as "insider" *(Chapter 14)*

You have just been commissioned by a prestigious journalism magazine to review your local newspaper (in no more than a page and a half). You should consider how well the paper fulfills its stated goals of service to the community, whether those goals are adequate, whether coverage of various community elements appears balanced, the editorial stance on local issues and the breadth, depth and quality of news coverage.

*Grade or Score*_____ *Name/Date*_____

Exercise 49 "Eds" and "op-eds" *(Chapter 14)*

One of the easier ways to learn to write opinion is to oppose an already formulated opinion. It helps to focus the argument and make the expression tightly organized and concise.

Pick any editorial from the local newspaper and write an editorial opposing whatever stand the paper has taken. Your actual opinions aren't important; you are practicing the technique of reasoned argument.

Grade or Score_____   Name/Date_____

Exercise 50   Editorials: The last word   (Chapter 14)

Editorials that succeed depend as much on the mastery of relevant facts as on the skillful phrasing of argument. Sound research produces good editorials. And good editorials are statements by an *institution*, not an *individual*. The editorial writer is essentially anonymous; the newspaper or the broadcast station "writes" the editorial.

As your organization's spokesperson, compose an editorial of no more than one and a half pages, urging action by your readers on one of the following topics:

1. The national defense budget
2. Federal social welfare programs
3. Your state's funding for higher education